FAVORITE
BASEBALL
★ TEAMS ★

MINNESOTA
TWINS

BY K. C. KELLEY

The Child's World®

Published by The Child's World®
1980 Lookout Drive • Mankato, MN 56003-1705
800-599-READ • www.childsworld.com

ACKNOWLEDGMENTS
The Child's World®: Mary Berendes,
    Publishing Director
The Design Lab: Kathleen Petelinsek, Design
Shoreline Publishing Group, LLC: James
    Buckley Jr., Production Director

PHOTOS
Cover: Focus on Baseball
Interior: All by Focus on Baseball except: AP/Wide
World: 8, 10, 16, 18, 22 (2)

LIBRARY OF CONGRESS
CATALOGING-IN-PUBLICATION DATA
Kelley, K. C.
  Minnesota Twins / by K.C. Kelley.
    p. cm. — (Favorite baseball teams)
  Includes index.
  ISBN 978-1-60253-379-0 (library bound : alk. paper)
  1. Minnesota Twins (Baseball team)—History—
Juvenile literature. I. Title. II. Series.
  GV875.M55K42 2010
  796.357'6409776579—dc22   2009039450

Printed in the United States of America
Mankato, Minnesota
November 2009
F11460

On the cover: Joe Mauer, Catcher

CONTENTS

Go, Twins!

Twins fans are some of the loudest in baseball! Their cheers fill the team's ballpark in Minneapolis, Minnesota. The Twins have had some great players to cheer for, too. And they've brought home two **World Series** titles for their fans. In 2010, the team celebrates its 50th season in Minnesota. Let's meet the Twins!

Star catcher Joe Mauer rounds second base on his way to scoring ▶ another run for the Twins!

Who Are the Twins?

The Minnesota Twins are a team in baseball's American League (A.L.). The A.L. joins with the National League to form Major League Baseball. The Twins play in the Central Division of the A.L. The division winners get to play in the league playoffs. The playoff winners from the two leagues face off in the World Series. The Twins have won two World Series championships.

◀ A trio of Twins celebrate a big win for Minnesota!

Where They Came From

The Minnesota Twins are sort of new . . . and sort of old. In 1901, the Washington Senators began to play. They were really bad for a long time! They did win the World Series in 1924. Except for that, they lost—a lot! In 1961, the team moved from Washington D.C. to Minnesota and got a new name: the Twins. They got their name from the "twin cities" of Minneapolis and St. Paul. The team tried to put their Washington days behind them. The Minnesota fans loved their new team!

Big Frank Howard was a powerful hitter for the Senators in the 1960s. ▶

Who They Play

The Minnesota Twins play 162 games each season. That includes 18 games against the other teams in their division, the A.L. Central. The Twins have won five A.L. Central championships. The other Central teams are the Chicago White Sox, the Cleveland Indians, the Detroit Tigers, and the Kansas City Royals. Minnesota's games against the White Sox are always exciting! The Twins also play some teams from the National League. Their N.L. **opponents** change every year.

◀ Wham! A solid slide by a Twins player knocked over this White Sox player at second base.

Where They Play

A brand-new stadium was built for the Twins' 2010 season. It's called Target Field. A "Tradition Wall" in the ballpark will list every player in Twins' history. Target Field does not have a roof. Fans didn't want a roof on the new stadium. Why? Because from 1982 through 2009, the Twins played indoors. Their home was the Hubert Humphrey Metrodome. Its white roof made it look like a giant marshmallow! People wanted to watch the team play outside instead.

Here's Target Field under construction. The builders were getting it ready ▶ for the 2010 season.

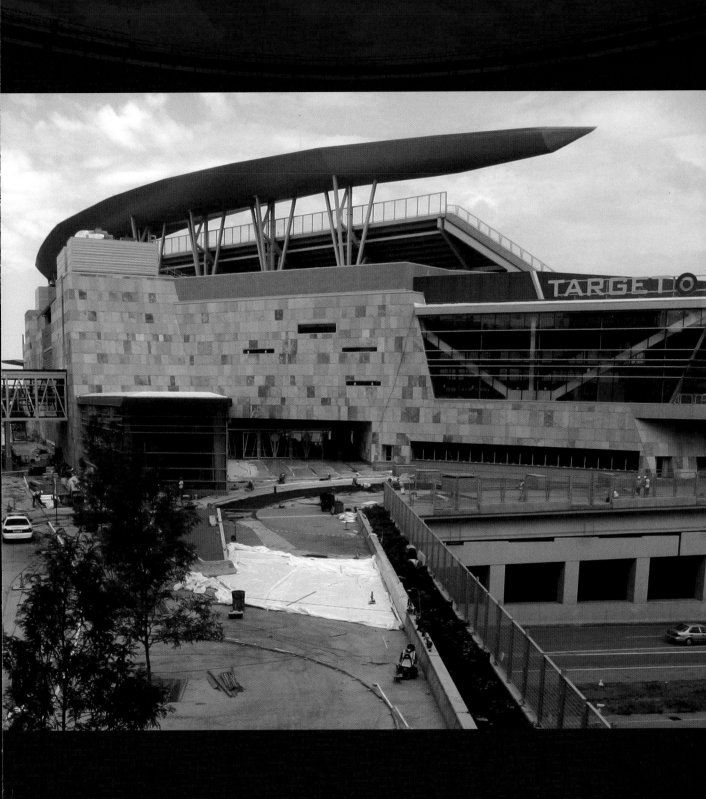

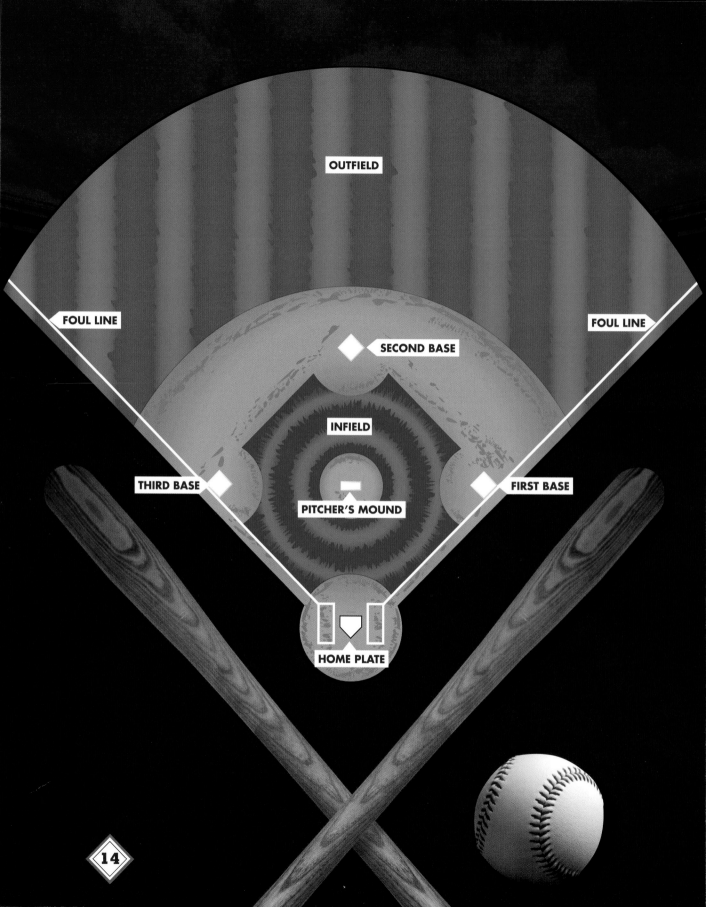

OUTFIELD

FOUL LINE

FOUL LINE

SECOND BASE

INFIELD

THIRD BASE

FIRST BASE

PITCHER'S MOUND

HOME PLATE

14

The Baseball Diamond

Baseball games are played on a diamond. Four bases form this diamond shape. The bases are 90 feet (27 m) apart. The area around the bases is called the **infield**. At the center of the infield is the pitcher's mound. The grass area beyond the bases is called the **outfield**. White lines start at **home plate** and go toward the outfield. These are the foul lines. Baseballs hit outside these lines are out of play. The outfield walls are about 300–450 feet (91–137 m) from home plate.

Big Days!

The Twins have had some great seasons in their history. Here are three of the best:

1965: In only their fifth season in Minnesota, the Twins made it to the World Series. They lost to the Dodgers in seven games. Still, it was a big move for a young team.

1987: A huge upset! The Twins beat the mighty St. Louis Cardinals to win their first World Series.

1991: In one of the best World Series ever, the Twins won a tough battle over the Atlanta Braves. Game 7 took 10 innings. The Twins won on a single by Gene Larkin that scored Dan Gladden . . . and the celebration started!

Star outfielder Kirby Puckett celebrated the Twins' 1987 World Series win . . . ▸ with his mom!

Tough Days!

Not every season can end with a World Series win. Here are some of the toughest seasons in the team's history:

1904: The Washington Senators had a lot of tough years. This was the worst. The team lost 113 of their 151 games!

1959: The Senators finished in last place in the American League. They were used to it by then. It was their third straight season in the bottom spot!

1990: They'd won the World Series only three years before. But this year, they finished last in their division.

◀ The Senators played in Griffith Stadium in Washington D.C. from 1911 to 1960.

Meet the Fans

Minnesota fans like to think they help
their team win. When they cheered inside the big
Metrodome, the noise bothered opponents. It was a
hard place to play the Twins, thanks to their noisy
fans. In their new ballpark, will Twins fans be as
loud? They'll certainly give it their best shot!

Can you guess which Twins star these young fans like the best? ▶

Walter Johnson, Pitcher

Heroes Then . . .

The Senators had one of the greatest pitchers of all time. Walter Johnson was called "The Big Train" for his super-fast pitching. He won 417 games, the second-most ever. He was one of the first five players chosen for the **Baseball Hall of Fame** in 1936. Many years later, slugger Harmon Killebrew helped the Twins reach the World Series in 1965. He had 573 career homers. In the 1960s and 1970s, infielder Rod Carew won seven A.L. batting titles! Outfielder Kirby Puckett had more hits than any big-league player in the 1990s. A great **defender** and **clutch** hitter, he helped the Twins win two World Series.

◀ Kirby Puckett was one of the most popular players in baseball during his great career. Inset: Walter Johnson threw a blazing fastball.

Heroes Now . . .

The Twins have two of the best young hitters in the Major Leagues. Catcher Joe Mauer has already won two batting titles. No other catcher has ever even earned one! First baseman Justin Morneau was the 2006 A.L. **Most Valuable Player (MVP)**. He has played in three **All-Star Games**, too. The Twins' top pitchers are Scott Baker and Joe Nathan. Baker is a great young pitcher. Nathan is a **relief pitcher**. He is awesome at closing down opponents in the late innings.

Joe Mauer, Catcher

Justin Morneau, First Base

Scott Baker, Pitcher

BATTING HELMET

BATTING GLOVE

BAT

UNDERSHIRT

TEAM JERSEY

TEAM PANTS

CATCHER'S MITT

CATCHER'S MASK

CATCHER'S CHEST PROTECTOR

CATCHER'S SHIN GUARD

Joe Mauer, Catcher

BASEBALL CLEATS

Gearing Up

Baseball players all wear a team jersey and pants. They have to wear a team hat in the field and a helmet when batting. Take a look at Joe Mauer to see some other parts of a baseball player's uniform.

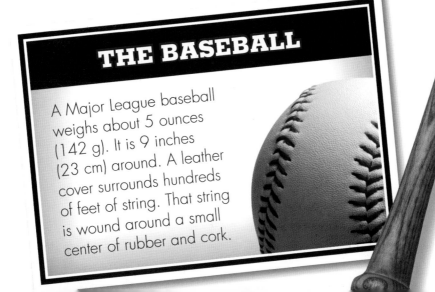

THE BASEBALL

A Major League baseball weighs about 5 ounces (142 g). It is 9 inches (23 cm) around. A leather cover surrounds hundreds of feet of string. That string is wound around a small center of rubber and cork.

SPORTS STATS

Here are some all-time career records for the Minnesota Twins. All the stats are through the 2009 season.

HOME RUNS

Harmon Killebrew, 559

Kent Hrbek, 293

RUNS BATTED IN

Harmon Killebrew, 1,540

Kent Hrbek, 1,086

BATTING AVERAGE

Rod Carew, .334

Heinie Manush, .328

WINS BY A PITCHER

Walter Johnson, 417

Jim Kaat, 190

STOLEN BASES

Clyde Milan, 495

Sam Rice, 346

WINS BY A MANAGER

Bucky Harris, 1,336

EARNED RUN AVERAGE

Walter Johnson, 2.17

Doc Ayers, 2.64

Glossary

All-Star Game a yearly game between the best players in each league

Baseball Hall of Fame a building in Cooperstown, New York, where baseball's greatest players are honored

clutch coming through in a tight spot, when the team really needs help

defender a player who is in the field, trying to keep the other team from scoring

home plate a five-sided rubber pad where batters stand to swing, and where runners touch base to score runs

infield the area around and between the four bases of a baseball diamond

manager the person who is in charge of the team and chooses who will bat and pitch

Most Valuable Player (MVP) a yearly award given to the top player in each league

opponents teams or players that play against each other

outfield the large, grass area beyond the infield of a baseball diamond

relief pitcher a pitcher who comes into a game to take another pitcher's place

World Series the Major League Baseball championship, played each year between the winners of the American and National Leagues

Find Out More

BOOKS

Buckley, James Jr. *Eyewitness Baseball*. New York: DK Publishing, 2010.

Stewart, Mark. *Minnesota Twins*. Chicago: Norwood House Press, 2008.

Teitelbaum, Michael. *Baseball*. Ann Arbor, MI: Cherry Lake Publishing, 2009.

Zuehlke, Jeffrey. *Joe Mauer*. Minneapolis: First Avenue Editions, 2008

WEB SITES

Visit our Web page for links about the Minnesota Twins and other pro baseball teams.

childsworld.com/links

Note to Parents, Teachers, and Librarians: We routinely verify our Web links to make sure they are safe, active sites—so encourage your readers to check them out!

Index

ABOUT THE AUTHOR

K.C. Kelley has written dozens of books on baseball and other sports for young readers. He has also been a youth baseball coach and called baseball games on the radio. His favorite team? The Boston Red Sox.